P9-BTN-099

Edited by
Sue Macy
and
Jane Gottesman

PLAY LIKE A GIRL

A Celebration of Women in Sports

Henry Holt and Company   /   New York

LIBRARY
FRANKLIN PIERCE COLLEGE
RINDGE, NH 03461

In memory of Joanne Winter,

an inspiration in her quiet confidence and pride

—S. M.

For Miss Mattos,

who taught us to just play

—J. G.

Henry Holt and Company, Inc., *Publishers since 1866*
115 West 18th Street, New York, New York 10011

Henry Holt is a registered trademark of Henry Holt and Company, Inc.
Copyright © 1999 by Sue Macy and Jane Gottesman
All rights reserved.
Published in Canada by Fitzhenry & Whiteside Ltd., 195 Allstate Parkway, Markham, Ontario L3R 4T8.

Library of Congress Cataloging-in-Publication Data
Play like a girl: a celebration of women in sports / (edited) by Sue Macy and Jane Gottesman.
p. cm.
Summary: Photographs and text portray the joy and dedication of
women participating in a variety of sports.
1. Sports for women—Juvenile literature. 2. Women athletes—Juvenile literature.
[1. Women athletes. 2. Sports for women.] I. Macy, Sue. II. Gottesman, Jane.
GV709.P53 1999 796'.082—dc21 98-47754

ISBN 0-8050-6071-5 / First Edition—1999
Designed by Meredith Baldwin
Printed in the United States of America on acid-free paper. ∞
1 2 3 4 5 6 7 8 9 10

The games consist of foot-races for maidens. The competitors are not all of the same age. The youngest run first, then those who come next in age, and finally the oldest of the maidens. This is how they run: Their hair hangs down, and they wear a tunic that reaches to a little above the knee, with the right shoulder bare as far as the breast. Like the men, they have the Olympic stadium reserved for their games, but the course is shortened for their races by about one sixth. To the winning maidens they give olive wreaths and a share of the cow sacrificed to [the goddess] Hera.

—*from* PAUSANIAS,
Description of Greece
(second century C.E.)

Every time, just before I take off in a race,
I always feel like I'm in a dream,

the kind of dream you have when you're sick with fever and feel all hot and weightless. . . . But once I spread my fingers in the dirt and crouch over for the Get on Your Mark, the dream goes and I am solid again and am telling myself, Squeaky, you must win, you must win, you are the fastest thing in the world, you can even beat your father up Amsterdam if you really try. And then I feel my weight coming back just behind my knees then down to my feet then into the earth and the pistol shot explodes in my blood and I am off and weightless again, flying past the other runners, my arms pumping up and down and the whole world is quiet except for the crunch as I zoom over the gravel in the track.

—TONI CADE BAMBARA,
from *"Raymond's Run"*

Breaststroke. . . .

There is no glide. No ease, or rest.

But there's this: **the rock and roll.**

From crown of head to lips, to hands, to hips,
and down. Like a dolphin, like a wave.
It's in the timing. In the hips. You want to flex
them, but not too much. Enough to generate
propulsion, yet without intruding. Enough for
motion, and optimal power. For the reach.
The pull. The thrust.

—JENIFER LEVIN,
from *The Sea of Light*

I'm intrigued by movement. . . .

As a volleyball coach I never see plays as
a series of x's and o's but as a sense of flow.

Movement rather than words
should be the prime communicator in any sport.

—MARY JO PEPPLER, Volleyball Player and Coach

In an attempt to focus my mind on absolutely nothing but

softball,

softball,

softball,

I squinted my eyes just slightly and tried to relax. My gaze settled casually upon that magical space above home plate, between the batter's knees and sweaty armpits, extending out toward the pitcher's mound to define the area where all the action in a game originates. It is the zone of emptiness that shimmers and shifts the most on hot, hazy, sweltering days. It is a column of air untouched, unbothered until a twentysomething-ounce aluminum shaft slices through it to meet or miss the offered pitch. It is the area I carefully patrol with my vision in the hopes of getting a good jump on any batted ball.

—KIMBERLY MILLER,
from *"Touching Goya: Thunder vs. Bombers 1992"*

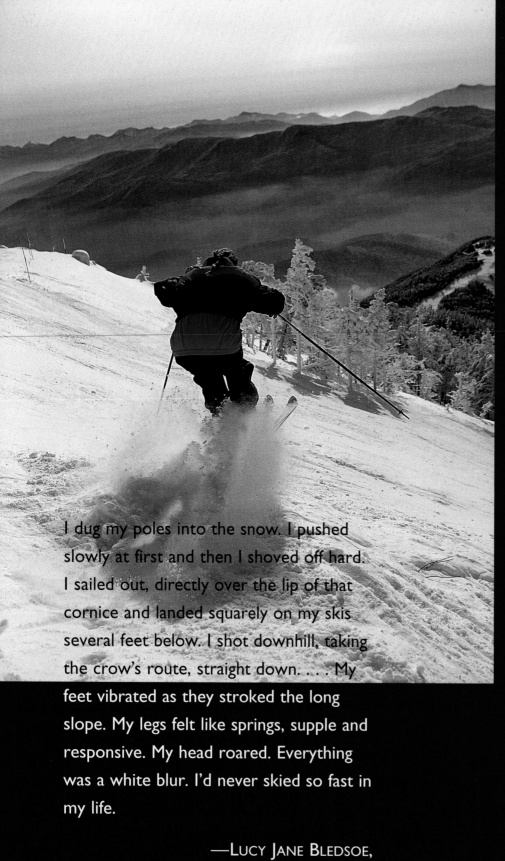

I dug my poles into the snow. I pushed
slowly at first and then I shoved off hard.
I sailed out, directly over the lip of that
cornice and landed squarely on my skis
several feet below. I shot downhill, taking
the crow's route, straight down. . . . My
feet vibrated as they stroked the long
slope. My legs felt like springs, supple and
responsive. My head roared. Everything
was a white blur. I'd never skied so fast in
my life.

—LUCY JANE BLEDSOE,
from *"Solo"*

First, there is the poetry of rowing. . . .
The motion of the stroke is grace itself, a fluid gesture that
propels the delicate shell inexorably forward. The sun is
wedging itself into the pale sky. A mist rises off the still water.
The shell barely intrudes. . . .

Rowers slide forward on their moving seats, drop their oars as
one into the water, catch the momentum and pass it on,
release the water and listen for its rush beneath the boat. They
repeat this gesture endlessly, captive to its rhythm. Quickly, the
water smoothes over any trace of their presence. And the
rowers themselves forget their separateness.

—LINDA LEWIS,
from *Water's Edge: Women Who Push
the Limits in Rowing, Kayaking & Canoeing*

The players looked bullet-proof,

the way athletes do in those rare slices of time when their minds
and bodies are working in perfect concert with their teammates'
minds and bodies.

We felt such an adrenaline rush, even on the bench, that I
completely understood mothers lifting cars off babies.

There is such power in the passion

that runs through your body at certain peak moments in your
life. This was what I was seeing now with these women. . . . I
had always carried in my mind a vision of how basketball should
look, as if it were art or a mathematical equation. There should
be balance and logic, a little bit of raw genius, some surprise and
beauty, and a seamless energy infusing it from beginning to end.
This was it.

—TARA VANDERVEER, Basketball Coach

Trying to articulate the zone is not easy because it's such an indescribable feeling. That moment doesn't happen often, and when it does happen, you feel like you're playing out of your head. . . .

You aren't feeling any tension or any pressure and physically your strokes are just flowing, every ball

you hit is going in. Emotionally you're really calm. There's no strain involved. It's a euphoric feeling. The feeling that whatever you touch turns to gold. Whatever you do, whatever decision you make on the court, whatever stroke or shot you try, you know it's going to work.

—CHRIS EVERT, Tennis Champion

The players . . . crouch, . . . bodies tense, ready to leap in any direction. Their eyes shift quickly from ball to opponent. A rush after the ball—two bodies crash in midair and tumble to the floor. The radiance in their eyes has changed to an almost insane glitter. The good-natured smiles are gone; faces are strained; sweat runs down into the players' eyes; mouths are half open, gasping for breath. It is a fight, and from the faces of the combatants, one would judge it to be a desperate fight. . . .

—MARJORIE BATEMAN,
College Physical Education Director
(condemning women's basketball in 1936)

I hoisted the pole up to my shoulders

and began to run down the path,

running into the light from the moon.

I picked up speed, thrust the pole into the cup,

and threw myself into the sky, into the still Delta night.

I sailed up and was clear and over the barrier.

I let go of the pole and began my fall, which

seemed to last a long, long time. It was like falling

through clear water. I dropped into the sawdust and

lay very still, waiting for them to reach me.

Sometimes I think whatever has happened since

has been of no real interest to me.

—ELLEN GILCHRIST,
from *In the Land of Dreamy Dreams*

Einstein was right. Time is relative. When you're winning, the game can't end soon enough, and every second on the clock moves forward as slowly as traffic caught behind a farmer on a tractor towing a corn planter. When you're losing, like tonight, it's over in seconds, a sudden skid on glare ice.

—MADELEINE BLAIS,
from *In These Girls, Hope Is a Muscle*

24

Like most competitors, I've lost more times than I've won. I've been defeated or rejected more times than I've finished first, ahead of the pack. But I've learned to see losses as painful but essential stumbles along an otherwise victorious path. I've learned not to let defeat diminish my core self-concept, my perception of myself as someone who wins.

—MARIAH BURTON NELSON,
from *Embracing Victory: Life Lessons in Competition and Compassion*

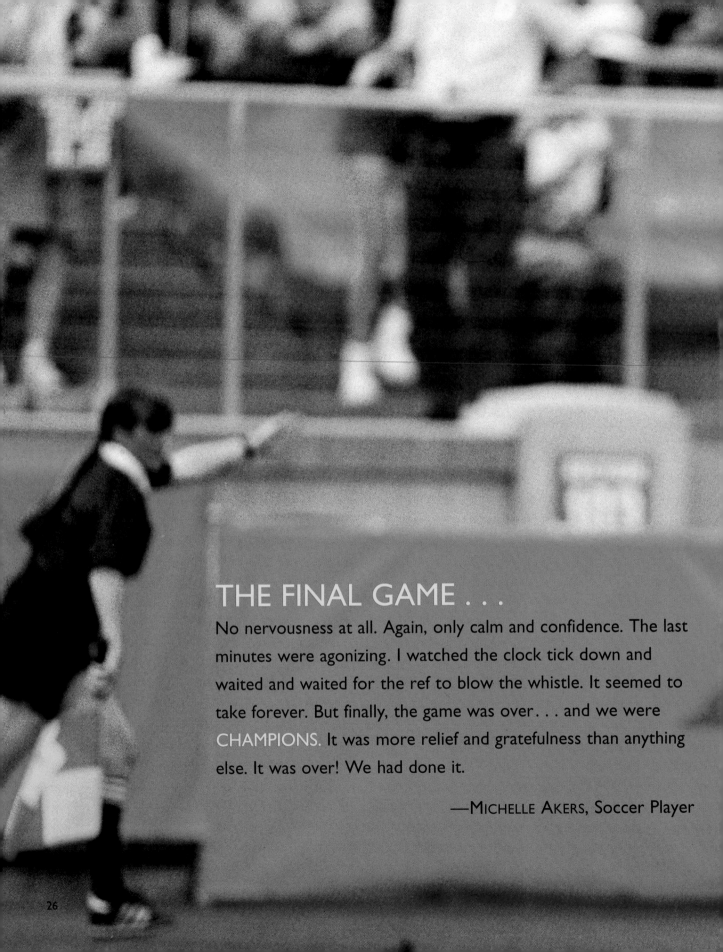

THE FINAL GAME . . .

No nervousness at all. Again, only calm and confidence. The last minutes were agonizing. I watched the clock tick down and waited and waited for the ref to blow the whistle. It seemed to take forever. But finally, the game was over. . . and we were CHAMPIONS. It was more relief and gratefulness than anything else. It was over! We had done it.

—MICHELLE AKERS, Soccer Player

In every race that I run and every line that I cross there is for me that Moment in Time—that winning moment of power and pleasure and grace. It's not a snapshot moment to be filed in the recesses of memory. It's a Technicolor moment of self-excedence and self-acceptance. It's a living moment of resource and possibility. It's a veritable encyclopedia of self-knowledge, a reference point from which to create and re-create that winning moment in all areas of my life.

And so, each year, I continue to cross the finish line. **With head thrown back and right arm raised in victory, I shout,** to the morning sky. It is one of the smallest words in the English language but also one of the largest. It is a word of infinite power and possibility.

—Zoe Koplowitz, Marathoner and MS Activist

Yes ''

It's 1 A.M. by the time the session winds down. Skaters drift into the parking lot . . . but Burnside lingers on the ramp.

She tries the same trick again and again, sometimes screaming in frustration and storming up the side of the ramp rather than using the steps. Her concentration is so intense you can almost hear it.

Watching, I remember asking her once what kept her going through all those years when she had so little encouragement, so few rewards. "I love skateboarding," she said simply. "I love skateboarding even when I have to skateboard with myself. I never expected anything to happen,

I did it for the love of it."

—JENNIFER EGAN,
from *"Girl Over Board"*

PERMISSIONS

p. 6: Excerpted from "Raymond's Run" from *Gorilla, My Love* by Toni Cade Bambara. Copyright © 1971 by Toni Cade Bambara. Used by permission of Random House, Inc.

p. 9: From *The Sea of Light* by Jenifer Levin. Copyright © 1993 by Jenifer Levin. Used by permission of Dutton, a division of Penguin Putnam Inc.

p. 10: From *Broken Patterns* by Pat Jordan. Copyright © 1974 by Pat Jordan. Used by permission of the author.

p. 13: From "Touching Goya: Thunder vs. Bombers 1992" by Kimberly Miller. Copyright © 1992 by Kimberly Miller. Used by permission of the author.

p. 14: Copyright © 1995 Lucy Jane Bledsoe. Excerpted from "Solo" from *Sweat: Stories and a Novella* by Lucy Jane Bledsoe, published by Seal Press.

p. 15: Copyright © 1992 Linda Lewis. Excerpted from *Water's Edge: Women Who Push the Limits in Rowing, Kayaking & Canoeing* by Linda Lewis, published by Seal Press.

p. 17: From *Shooting from the Outside* by Tara VanDerveer with Joan Ryan. Copyright © 1997 by Tara VanDerveer and Joan Ryan. By permission of Avon Books, Inc.

pp. 18–19: From *What Makes Winners Win*, written and compiled by Charlie Jones. Copyright © 1997 by Charlie Jones. Published by arrangement with Carol Publishing Group. A Birch Lane Press Book.

p. 20: From "Health Aspects of Girls' Basketball" by Marjorie Bateman. Copyright © 1936 by American Physical Education Association. Used by permission of National Association for Girls and Women in Sport; www.aahperd.org.

pp. 22–23: From *In the Land of Dreamy Dreams* by Ellen Gilchrist. Copyright © 1981 by Ellen Gilchrist. By permission of Little, Brown and Company.

p. 24: From *In These Girls, Hope Is a Muscle* by Madeleine Blais. Copyright © 1995 by Madeleine Blais. Used by permission of Grove/Atlantic, Inc.

p. 25: From *Embracing Victory: Life Lessons in Competition and Compassion* by Mariah Burton Nelson. Copyright © 1998 by Mariah Burton Nelson. By permission of William Morrow and Company, Inc.

p. 26: From *Standing Fast* by Michelle Akers and Tim Nash. Copyright © 1997 by JTC Sports, Inc., and Michelle Akers. Reprinted as adapted by Michelle Akers for her homepage at www.michelleakers.com. Used by permission of the author.

p. 29: From *Winning Spirit: Life Lessons Learned in Last Place* by Zoe Koplowitz. Copyright © 1997 by Zoe Koplowitz. Used by permission of Doubleday, a division of Bantam Doubleday Dell Publishing Group, Inc.

p. 31: From "Girl Over Board" by Jennifer Egan in *Condé Nast Sports for Women* (April 1998). Copyright © 1998 by Jennifer Egan. Used by permission of the author.

PHOTO CREDITS

p. 1: Colleen Snyder (left) and Christina Gilytin, University of California, Santa Barbara vs. Stanford, 1997 (Mathew Sumner).

p. 3: Women's 800-meter race, Olympic Sports Festival, 1995 (Rick Rickman).

p. 4: Triathletes, Berkeley, California, 1986 (Joan Bobkoff).

p. 5: Triathlete Amanda White (top), Palo Alto, California, 1996 (Meri Simon / *San Jose Mercury News*); Sakai Metcalf (bottom), Oakland, California, 1994 (Brant Ward).

p. 6: Evelyn Ashford, Olympic trials, 1992 (Cindy Collins).

p. 7: Rochelle Stevens, 4 x 400-meter relay, Olympic trials, 1996 (Cindy Collins).

p. 8: (David Burnett / CONTACT).

p. 11: Stacy Millichap, San Jose, California, 1998 (Meri Simon / *San Jose Mercury News*).

p. 12: U.S. Olympic Festival, 1991 (Paul J. Sutton / DUOMO).

p. 14: Whiteface Mountain, Adirondack Mountains, 1997 (Nancie Battaglia).

p. 15: The Vesper Boat Club, Schuylkill River, Philadelphia, 1987 (Marilyn A. Shapiro).

p. 16: Venus Lacey, Oakland, California, 1996 (Meri Simon / *San Jose Mercury News*).

p. 18–19: Martina Navratilova, 1991 (Chris Hamilton).

p. 21: Kara Wolters (left) and Katryna Gaither, New England Blizzard vs. San Jose Lasers, 1998 (Dan Krauss / *San Francisco Examiner*).

p. 22: Olympic trials, 1996 (Cindy Collins).

p. 24–25: Tasha Bradley (right), University of Nevada, Las Vegas vs. Stanford, 1991 (Meri Simon).

p. 26–27: Shannon MacMillan (left) and Kristine Lilly, Olympic Games, 1996 (Chris Cole / DUOMO).

p. 28: Monica Wetterstrom, Paralympics, 1992 (Eileen Langsley).

pp. 30–31: Cara-Beth Burnside, 1998 (copyright © A & C Anthology).

p. 32: Lacrosse players, Miss Porter's School, Farmington, Connecticut, 1997 (Frank Marchese).

FRANKLIN PIERCE COLLEGE LIBRARY

00126520

DATE DUE